# ALFRED'S BASIC UKULELE METHOD 1

## THE MOST POPULAR METHOD FOR LEARNING HOW TO PLAY

*For individual or class instruction*

RON MANUS

& L.C. HARNSBERGER

D1308258

Alfred Music Publishing Co., Inc.
P.O. Box 10003
Van Nuys, CA 91410-0003
alfred.com

 **Alfred Cares.** Contents printed on 100% recycled paper.

Book
ISBN-10: 0-7390-7349-4          ISBN-13: 978-0-7390-7349-0
Book and CD
ISBN-10: 0-7390-7352-4          ISBN-13: 978-0-7390-7352-0
Book and DVD
ISBN-10: 0-7390-7353-2          ISBN-13: 978-0-7390-7353-7
DVD
ISBN-10: 0-7390-7351-6          ISBN-13: 978-0-7390-7351-3
CD
ISBN-10: 0-7390-7350-8          ISBN-13: 978-0-7390-7350-6

2

# Contents

# Selecting Your Ukulele

Ukuleles come in different types and sizes. There are four basic sizes: soprano, concert, tenor, and baritone. The smallest is the soprano, and they get gradually larger, with the baritone being the largest.

**Soprano**     **Concert**     **Tenor**     **Baritone**

Soprano, concert, and tenor ukuleles are all tuned to the same notes, but the baritone is tuned differently. Each ukulele has a different sound. The soprano has a light, soft sound, which is what you expect when you hear a ukulele. The larger the instrument, the deeper the sound is. Some tenor ukuleles have six or even eight strings.

The soprano ukulele is the most common, but you can use soprano, concert, and four-string tenor ukuleles with this book. Because the baritone ukulele is tuned to the same notes as the top four strings of the guitar, you can use *Learn to Play Baritone Uke* (Alfred item 380) to start learning.

# The Parts of Your Ukulele

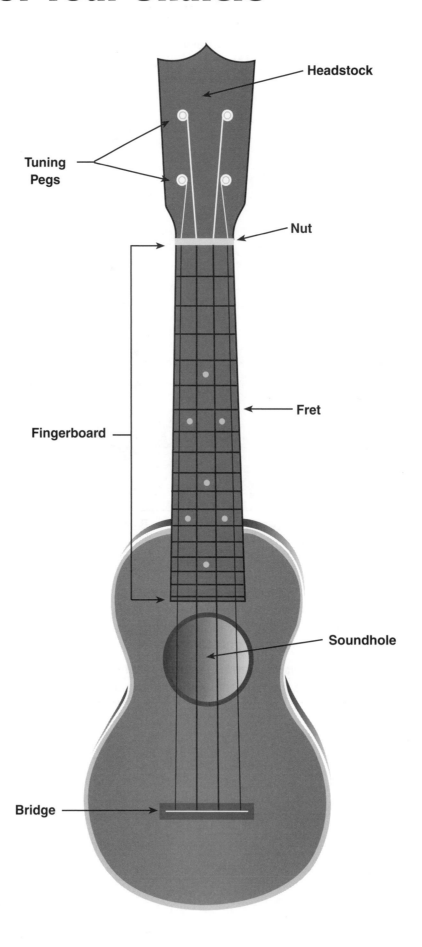

Headstock

Tuning Pegs

Nut

Fret

Fingerboard

Soundhole

Bridge

# How to Hold Your Ukulele

## Standing

Cradle the ukulele with your right arm by gently holding it close to your body. Your right hand should be free to strum it. Keep your left wrist away from the fingerboard. This allows your fingers to be in a better position to finger the chords.

## Sitting

Rest the ukulele gently on your thigh.

# The Right Hand: Strumming the Strings

To *strum* means to play the strings with your right hand by brushing quickly across them. There are two common ways of strumming the strings. One is with a pick, and the other is with your fingers.

## Strumming with a Pick

Hold the pick between your thumb and index finger. Hold it firmly, but don't squeeze it too hard.

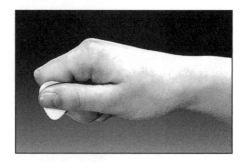

Strum from the 4th string (closest to the ceiling) to the 1st string (closest to the floor).

**Important:** Always strum by mostly moving your wrist, not just your arm. Use as little motion as possible. Start as close to the top strings as you can, and never let your hand move past the edge of the ukulele.

**Start near the top string.**

**Move mostly your wrist, not just your arm. Finish near the bottom string.**

## Strumming with Your Fingers

Decide if you feel more comfortable strumming with the side of your thumb or the nail of your index finger. The strumming motion is the same with the thumb or finger as it is when using the pick. Strum from the 4th string to the 1st string.

**Strumming with the thumb.**

**Strumming with the index finger.**

# Using Your Left Hand

## Hand Position

Learning to use your left-hand fingers easily starts with a good hand position. Place your hand so your thumb rests comfortably in the middle of the back of the neck. Position your fingers on the front of the neck as if you are gently squeezing a ball between them and your thumb. Keep your elbow in and your fingers curved.

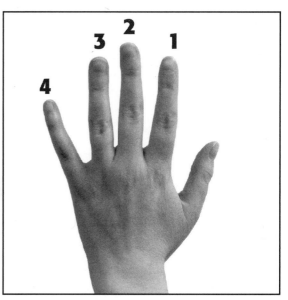

**Keep elbow in and fingers curved.**

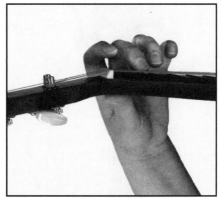

**Like gently squeezing a ball between your fingers and thumb.**

## Placing a Finger on a String

When you press a string with a left-hand finger, make sure you press firmly with the tip of your finger and as close to the fret wire as you can without actually being right on it. Short fingernails are important! This will create a clean, bright tone.

**RIGHT**
**Finger pressed the string down near the fret without actually being on it.**

**WRONG**
**Finger is too far from fret wire; tone is "buzzy" and indefinite.**

**WRONG**
**Finger is on top of fret wire; tone is muffled and unclear.**

# How to Tune Your Ukulele

Make sure your strings are wound properly around the tuning pegs. They should go from the inside to the outside, as in the picture.

Tuning a tuning peg clockwise makes the pitch lower. Turning a tuning peg counter-clockwise makes the pitch higher. Be sure not to tune the strings too high because they could break!

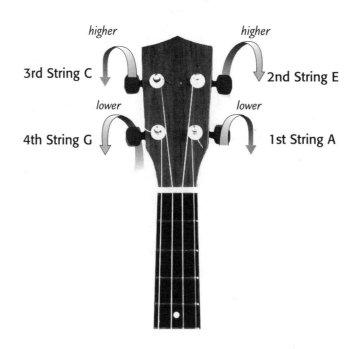

*higher*  *higher*

3rd String C  2nd String E

*lower*  *lower*

4th String G  1st String A

## Important:

Always remember that the string closest to the floor is the 1st string. The one closest to the ceiling is the 4th string.

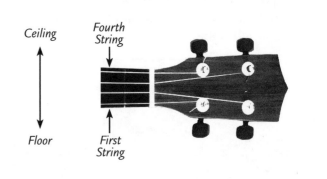

*Ceiling*  Fourth String

*Floor*  First String

## Tuning with the CD or DVD  **Track 1**

To use the CD, play track 1. Listen to the directions and match each of your ukulele's strings to the corresponding pitches.

To use the DVD, go to the "Scenes" menu and click "Tuning." Follow the directions, and listen carefully to get your ukulele in tune.

# Tuning the Ukulele to Itself without the CD or DVD

When your 1st string is in tune, you can tune the rest of the strings just using the ukulele alone.
First, tune the 1st string to A on the piano, and then follow the instructions to get the ukulele in tune.

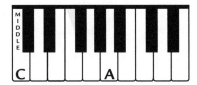

Press fret 5 of string 2 and tune it to the pitch of string 1 (A).

Press fret 4 or string 3 and tune it to the pitch of string 2 (E).

Press fret 2 of string 4 and tune it to the pitch of string 1 (A).

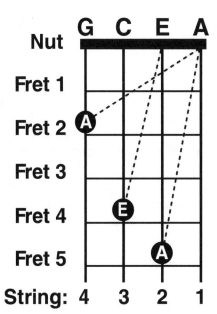

# Pitch Pipes and Electronic Tuners

If you don't have a piano available, buying an electronic tuner or pitch pipe is recommended.
The salesperson at your music store can show you how to use them.

# Getting Acquainted with Music

Musical sounds are indicated by symbols called *notes*. Their time value is determined by their color (white or black) and by stems or flags attached to the note.

## The Staff

The notes are named after the first seven letters of the alphabet (A–G), endlessly repeated to embrace the entire range of musical sound. The name and pitch of the note is determined by its position on five horizontal lines, and the spaces between, called the *staff*.

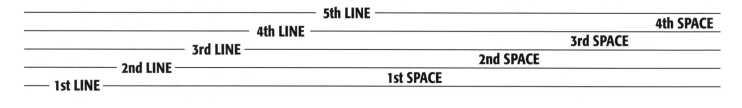

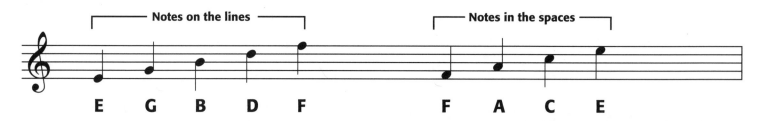

## Measures

Music is divided into equal parts called *measures*. One measure is divided from another by a *bar line*.

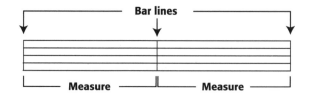

## Clefs

During the evolution of musical notation, the staff had from 2 to 20 lines, and symbols were invented to locate certain lines and the pitch of the note on that line. These symbols are called *clefs*.

Music for ukulele is written in the *G clef* or *treble clef*.
Originally, the Gothic letter G was used on a four-line staff to establish the pitch of G.

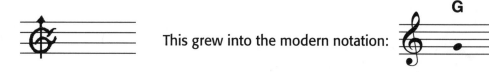

This grew into the modern notation:

# Reading TAB

All the music in this book is written two ways: in standard music notation and TAB.

Below each standard music staff you'll find a four-line TAB staff. Each line represents a string of the ukulele, with the 1st string at the top and the 4th string at the bottom.

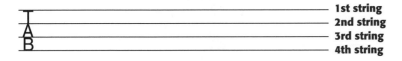

Numbers placed on the TAB lines tell you which fret to play. An o means to play the string open (not fingered).

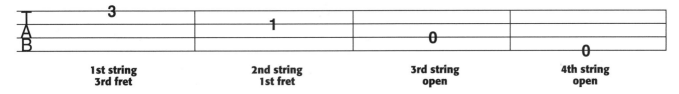

By glancing at the TAB, you can immediately tell where to play a note. Although you can't tell exactly what the rhythm is from the TAB, the horizontal spacing of the numbers gives you a strong hint about how long or short the notes are to be played.

# Chord Diagrams

Chord diagrams are used to indicate fingering for chords. The example here means to place your 1st finger on the 1st fret, 1st string, then strum all four strings. The o symbols on the 2nd, 3rd, and 4th strings indicate to play them open (not fingered).

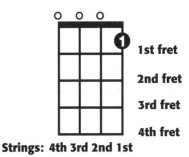

# The First String A

Track 2

**OPEN STRING**
**(not fingered)**

**2nd FRET**

**3rd FRET**

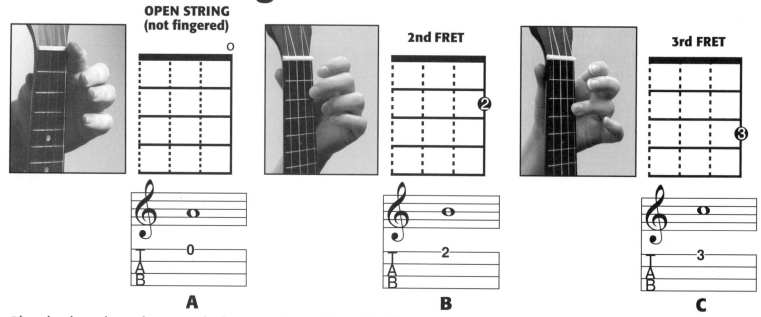

A            B            C

Play slowly and evenly. Use only down-strokes, indicated by ⊓.
The symbol ○ over a note means *open string*. Do not finger.

## Playing with A, B, C

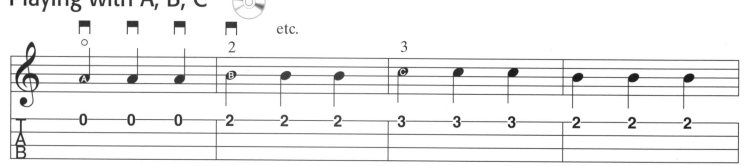

DOUBLE BAR LINE

USED TO SIGNAL THE
END OF THE PIECE

# Extra Credit

Make sure to place your left-hand fingers as close to the fret wires as possible without touching them. When you play the B on the 2nd fret and follow it with the C on the 3rd fret, keep your 2nd finger down. You will only hear the C, but when you go back to the B, it will sound smooth.

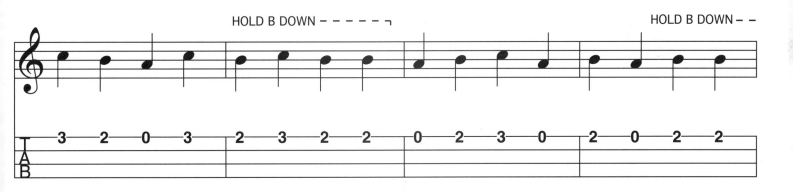

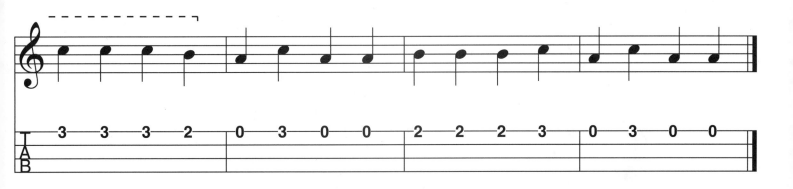

# Sound-Off: How to Count Time

## 4 Kinds of Notes

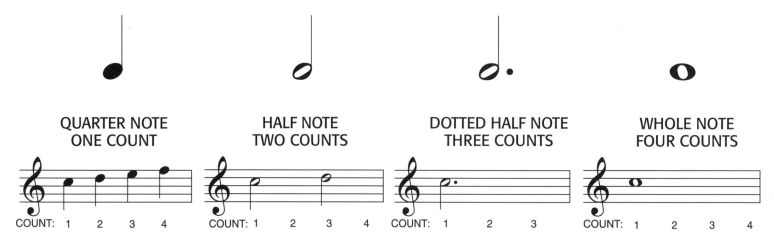

| QUARTER NOTE ONE COUNT | HALF NOTE TWO COUNTS | DOTTED HALF NOTE THREE COUNTS | WHOLE NOTE FOUR COUNTS |

## Time Signatures

Each piece of music has numbers at the beginning called a *time signature*. These numbers tell us how to count time. The TOP NUMBER tells us how many counts are in each measure. The BOTTOM NUMBER tells us what kind of note gets one count.

FOUR COUNTS TO A MEASURE

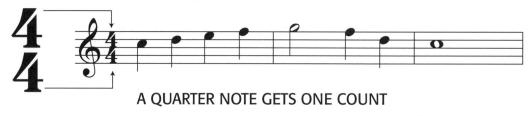

A QUARTER NOTE GETS ONE COUNT

THREE COUNTS TO A MEASURE

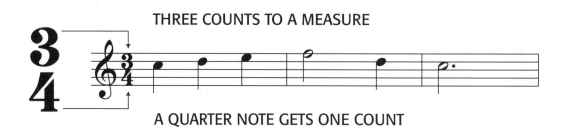

A QUARTER NOTE GETS ONE COUNT

TWO COUNTS TO A MEASURE

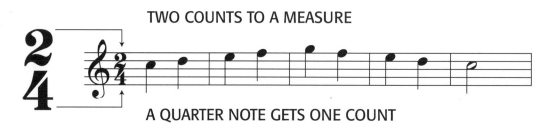

A QUARTER NOTE GETS ONE COUNT

**Important:** Go back and fill in the missing time signatures of the songs already learned.

# Repeat Signs

This music uses *repeat signs*. The double dots inside the double bars tell you that everything in between those double bars is to be repeated.

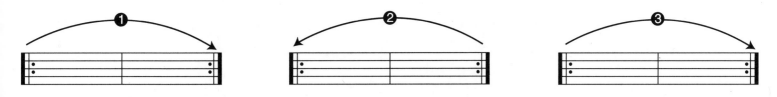

The best way to learn all the songs and exercises is to listen to the recording first so that you can hear exactly what is going to happen. Follow along in the music as you listen. Then, enjoy playing along.

## 1st String Blues       Track 5

# The Second String E

**NOTES YOU'VE LEARNED SO FAR**

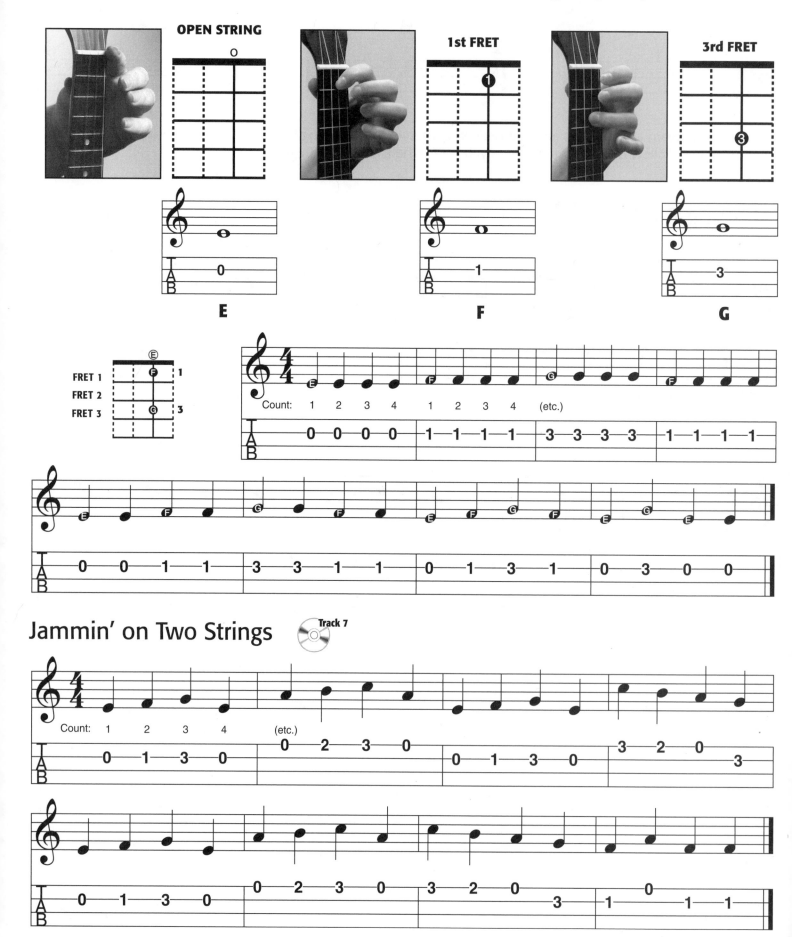

# Hot Cross Buns

**Track 8**

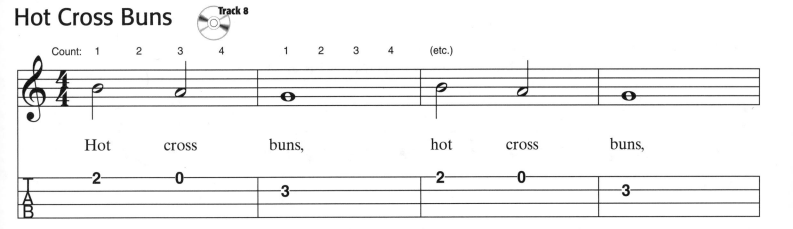

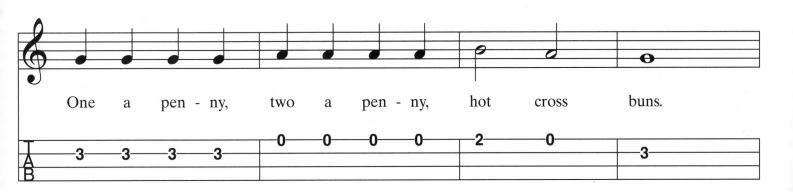

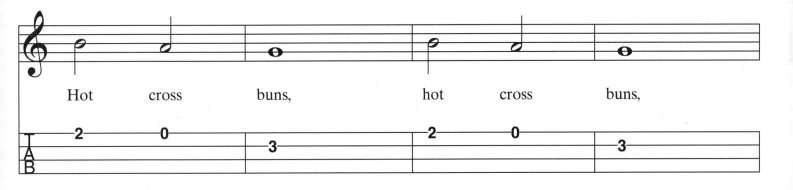

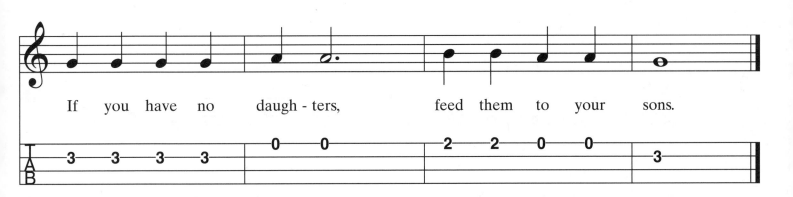

18

# Blues in C  Track 9

If the teacher wvishes to play along with the student, the chord symbols above each staff may be used for a teacher-student duet. These chords are not to be played by the student.

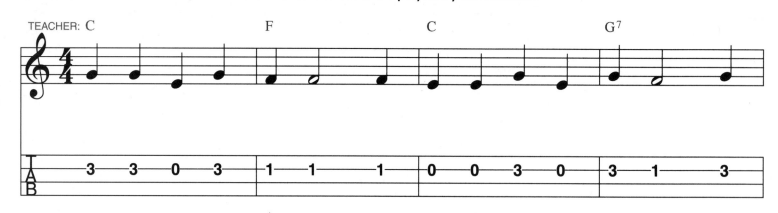

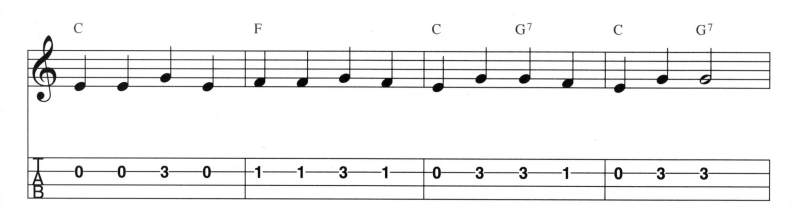

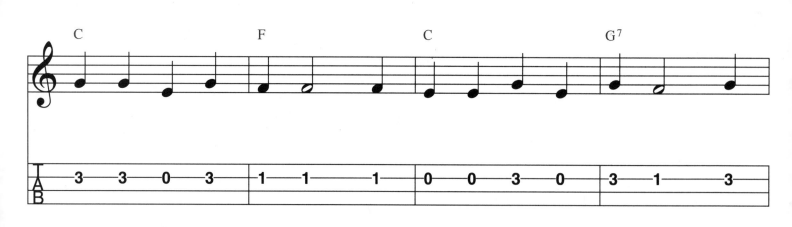

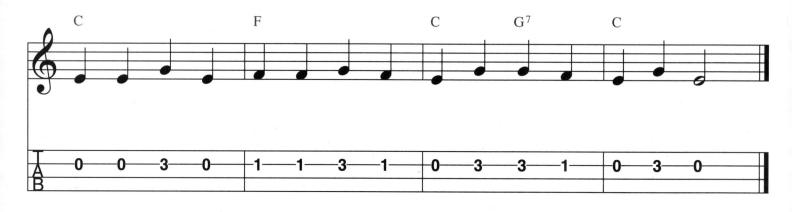

## Rockin' Uke

# The Third String C  Track 11

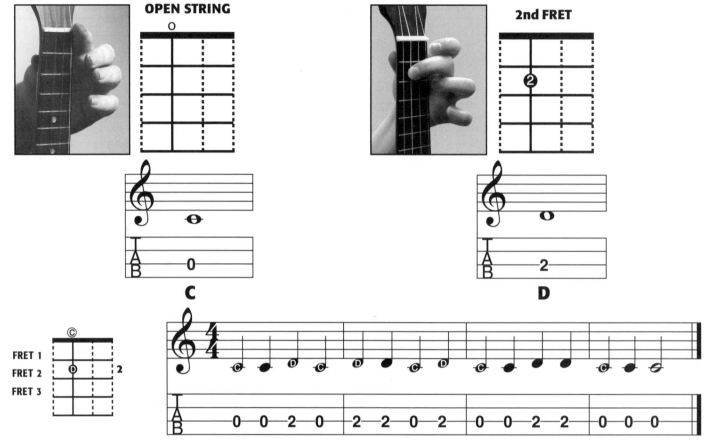

**OPEN STRING**

**2nd FRET**

**C**

**D**

## Jammin' on Three Strings  Track 12

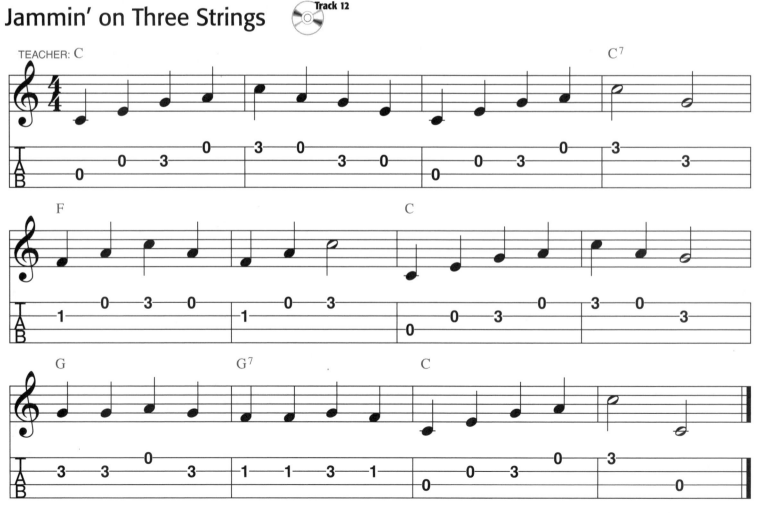

# Largo

(from the *New World Symphony*)

Antonin Dvořák

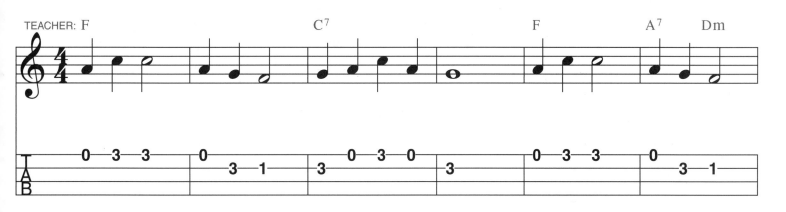

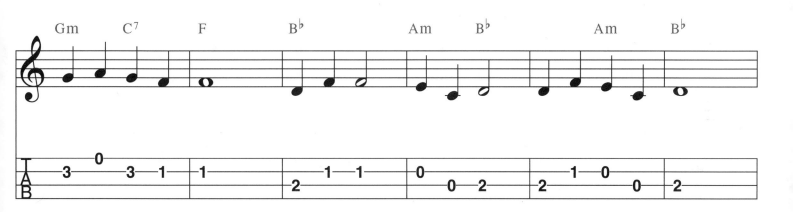

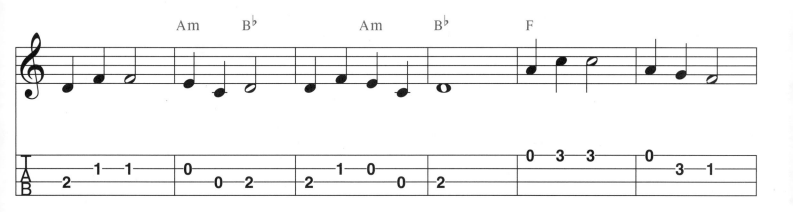

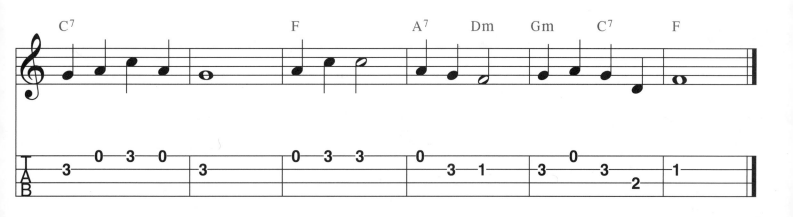

# Jingle Bells

 **Track 14**

TEACHER: C

Jin - gle bells! Jin - gle bells! Jin - gle all the way!

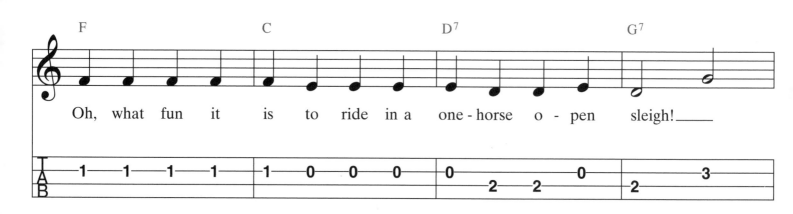

Oh, what fun it is to ride in a one - horse o - pen sleigh!___

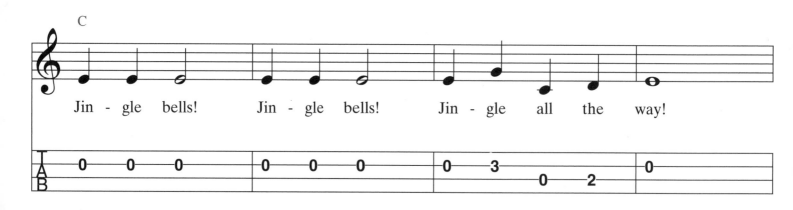

Jin - gle bells! Jin - gle bells! Jin - gle all the way!

Oh, what fun it is to ride in a one - horse o - pen sleigh!___

# Beautiful Brown Eyes

 Track 15

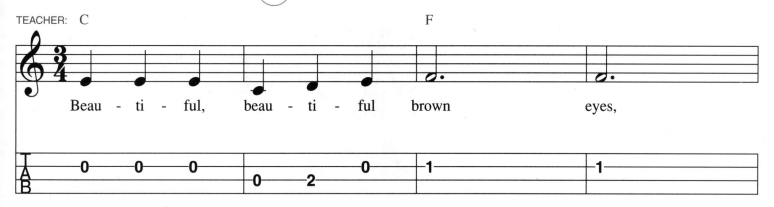

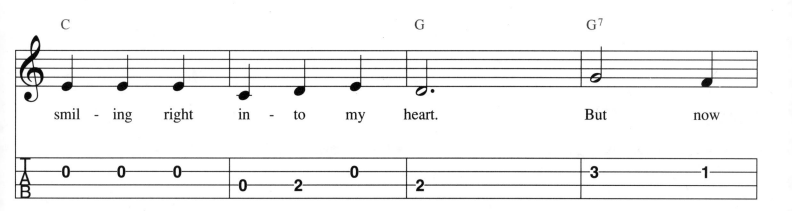

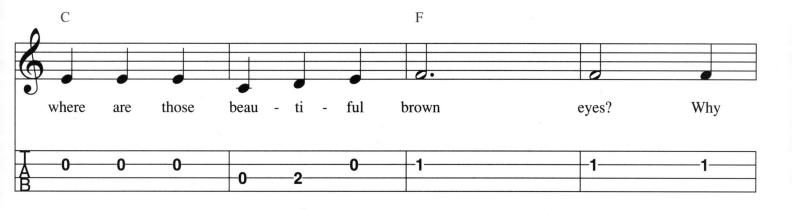

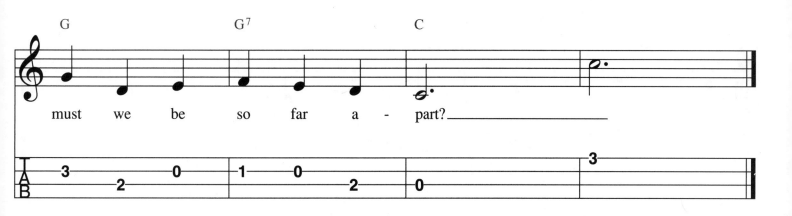

# Introducing B-flat  Track 16

A *flat* ♭ lowers a note a half step. B♭ is played one fret lower than the note B. When a flat note appears in a measure, it is still flat until the end of that measure.

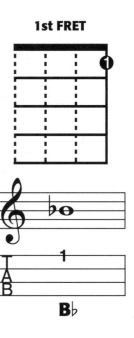

**1st FRET**

**B♭**

## Aura Lee  Track 17

This old American folk song was later recorded by Elvis Presley and called "Love Me Tender."

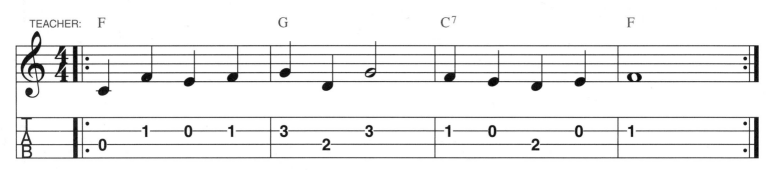

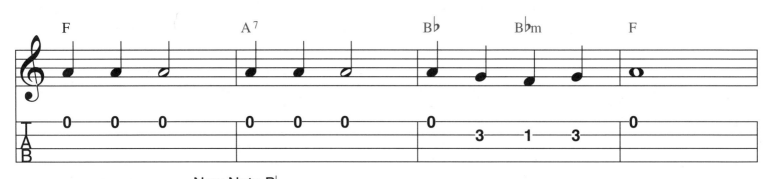

New Note B♭

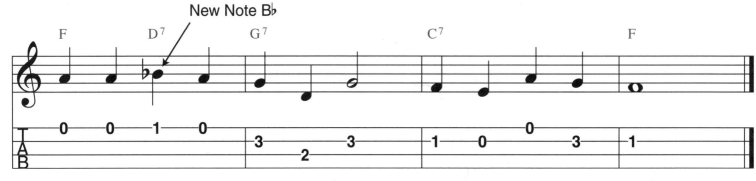

# Three-String Boogie  Track 18

This song uses all the notes you have learned. Don't forget to listen to the audio on the CD or DVD first!

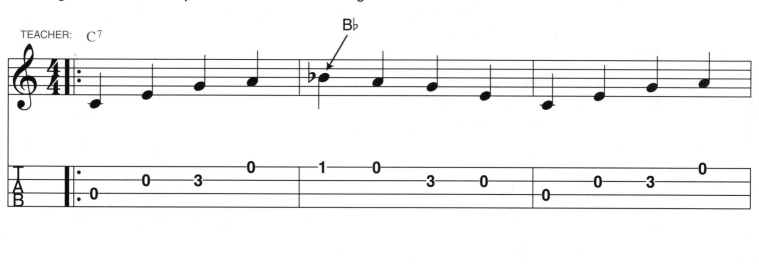

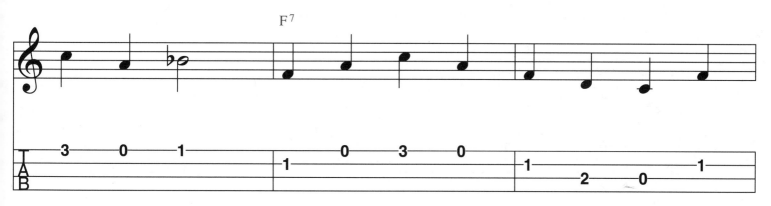

# Tempo Signs

A *tempo sign* tells you how fast to play the music. Below are the three most common tempo signs, which are Italian words. In some music, you will see tempo signs written in English.

**Andante** ("ahn-DAHN-teh") means to play slow.

**Moderato** ("moh-deh-RAH-toh") means to play moderately.

**Allegro** ("ah-LAY-groh") means to play fast.

| | |
|---|---|
|  | ## Quarter Rest |
| | This sign indicates silence for one count. For a clearer effect, you may stop the sound of the strings by touching the strings lightly with the heel of the right hand. |

## Three-Tempo Rockin' Uke   Track 19

Play three times: first time **Andante**, second time **Moderato**, third time **Allegro**.

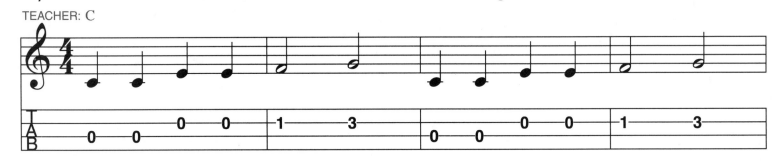

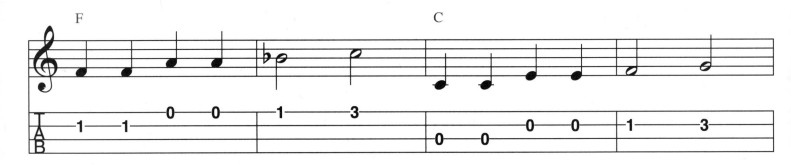

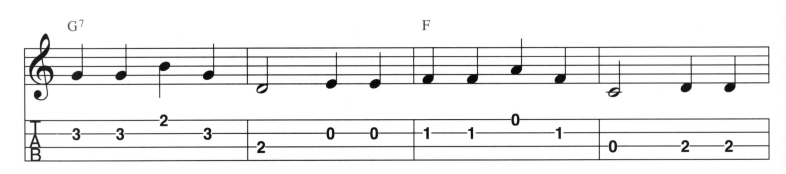

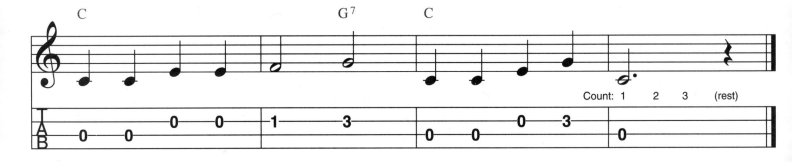

# The C7 Chord

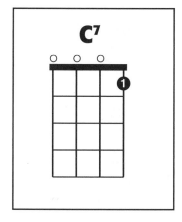

o = open string

- - - - - - - - - = string is not played

Place your 1st finger in position, then play one string at a time.

Play all four
strings together:

 + 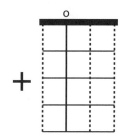 + 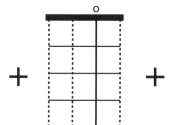 + 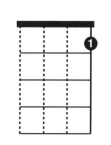 =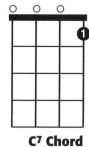

C⁷ Chord

Play slowly and evenly. Each slash mark ∕ means to repeat the previous chord. Strum downward
for each chord name and slash mark. Use your finger or a pick. The chord name is repeated in each measure.

1. $\begin{array}{c} 2 \\ 4 \end{array}$ C⁷ ∕ | C⁷ ∕ | C⁷ ∕ | C⁷ ∕ | C⁷ ∕ | C⁷ ∕ ‖

2. $\begin{array}{c} 3 \\ 4 \end{array}$ C⁷ ∕ ∕ | C⁷ ∕ ∕ | C⁷ ∕ ∕ | C⁷ ∕ ∕ ‖

3. $\begin{array}{c} 4 \\ 4 \end{array}$ C⁷ ∕ ∕ ∕ | C⁷ ∕ ∕ ∕ | C⁷ ∕ ∕ ∕ ‖

# The F Chord  Track 22

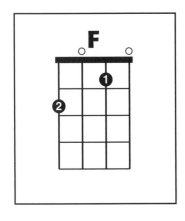

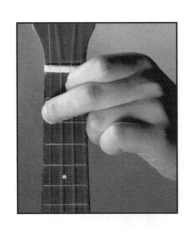

**ANOTHER CHORD ON THIS PAGE**

**C⁷**

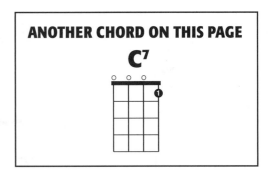

Place your 1st and 2nd fingers in position, then play one string at a time.

Play all four strings together:

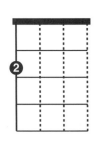 + 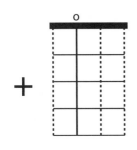 + 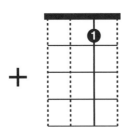 + 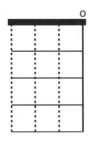 =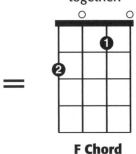

**F Chord**

 Track 23

1.

2.

3.

 Track 24

Once you can play both the F and C7 chords clearly, try combining them as in the following exercises.

1. 

HOLD

2. 

COUNT: 1 REST REST

3.

# Good Night Ladies

Track 25 — Vocals & Chords  Track 26 — Chords only

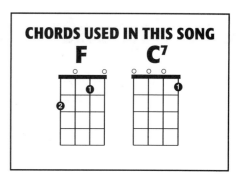

CHORDS USED IN THIS SONG
F  C7

For this song and most of the rest of the songs in this book, you can play either the melody or chords. Your teacher can play the part you aren't playing, or you can play along with the CD or DVD.

**Moderato**

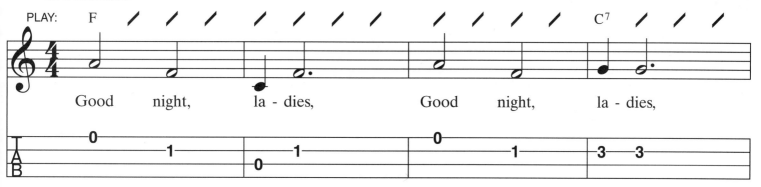

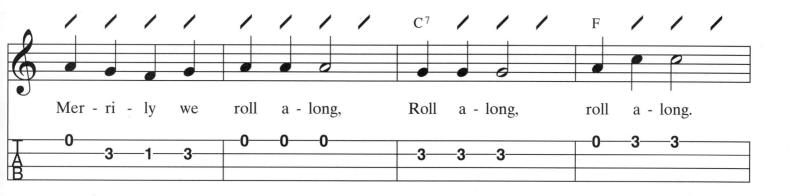

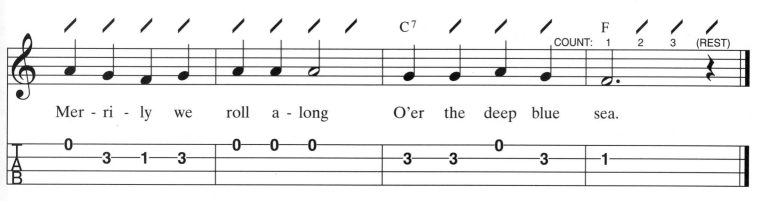

# Key Signatures

The *key signature* at the beginning of a piece tells you when a note is played as a flat note throughout the piece. In "Down in the Valley," each B is played as B-flat.

## Ties

This curved line is called a *tie*. It connects two or more notes and ties them together. Play or sing the note once and hold it for the value of both (or more) tied notes. In TAB, a tied note is shown as a number in parentheses. Do not pick the note again.

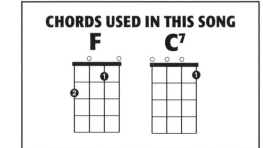

**CHORDS USED IN THIS SONG**
F    C⁷

## Down in the Valley

**Track 27** Vocals & Chords    **Track 28** Chords only

Key Signature: remember to play each B one half step lower.

32

# Ode to Joy

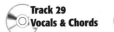

Theme from Beethoven's Ninth Symphony

Moderato

# The C Chord

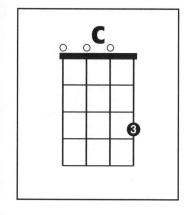

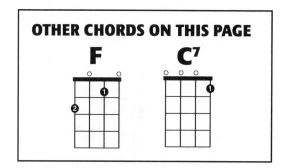

Place your 3rd finger in position, then play one string at a time.

Play all four strings together:

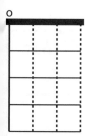 + 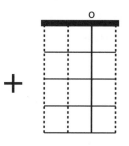 + 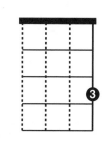 + 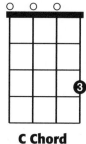 =

**C Chord**

Play slowly and evenly.

Now try these exercise. They combine all the chords you know.

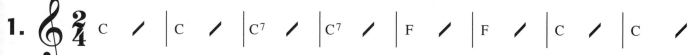

34

# Incomplete Measures

Not all pieces of music begin on the first beat. Sometimes, music begins with an incomplete measure called a *pickup*. If the pickup is one beat, often the last measure will only have three beats in $\frac{4}{4}$, or two beats in $\frac{3}{4}$.

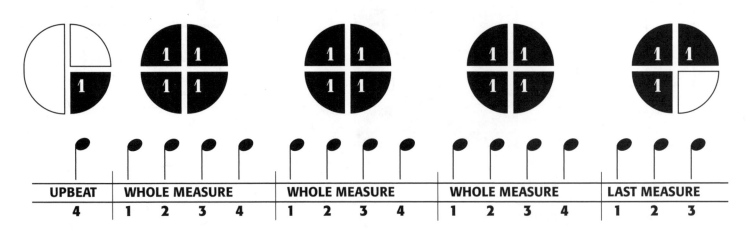

| UPBEAT | WHOLE MEASURE | | | | WHOLE MEASURE | | | | WHOLE MEASURE | | | | LAST MEASURE | | |
|---|---|---|---|---|---|---|---|---|---|---|---|---|---|---|---|
| 4 | 1 | 2 | 3 | 4 | 1 | 2 | 3 | 4 | 1 | 2 | 3 | 4 | 1 | 2 | 3 |

Track 34
Vocals & Chords

Track 35
Chords only

**CHORDS USED IN THIS SONG**
F    C    C⁷

## A-Tisket, A-Tasket

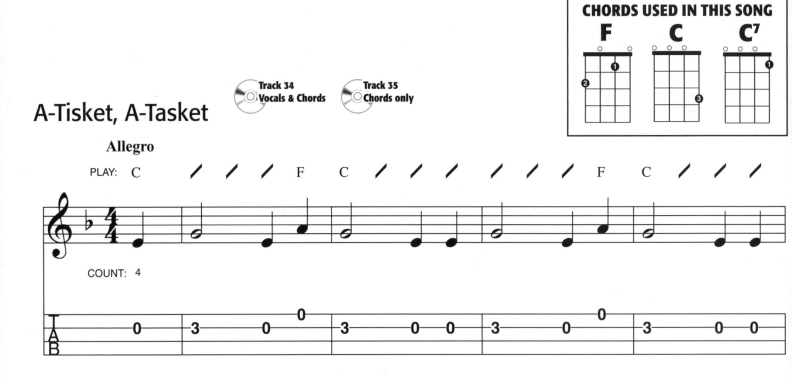

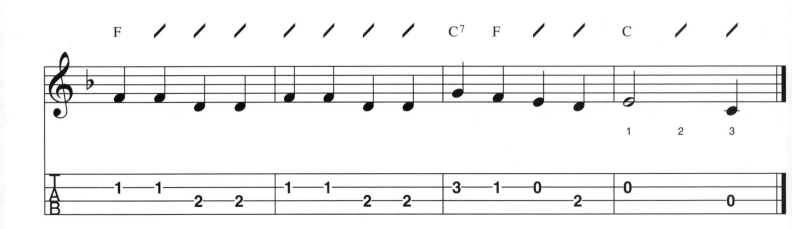

# Eighth Notes

*Eighth notes* are black notes with a flag added to the stem: ♪ or ♩ .

Two or more eighth notes are written with beams: ♫ or ♫ , ♬ or ♬ .

Each eighth note receives one half beat.

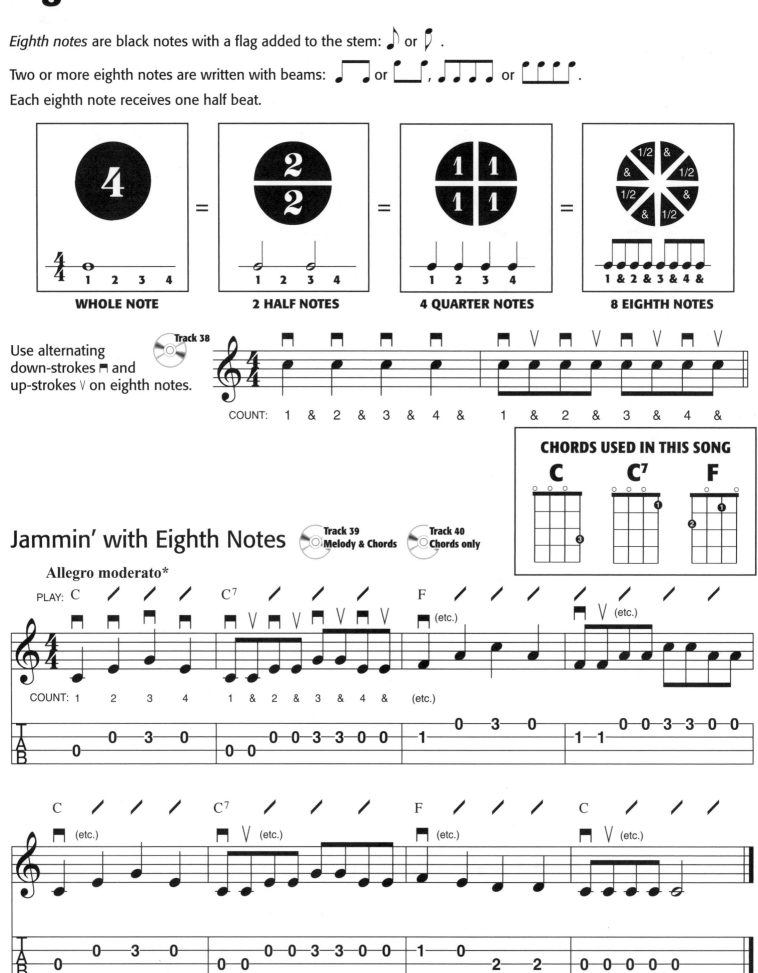

Use alternating down-strokes ⊓ and up-strokes ∨ on eighth notes.

**CHORDS USED IN THIS SONG**
C    C⁷    F

## Jammin' with Eighth Notes

*Allegro moderato*

*Allegro moderato means moderately fast.

# Go Tell Aunt Rhody

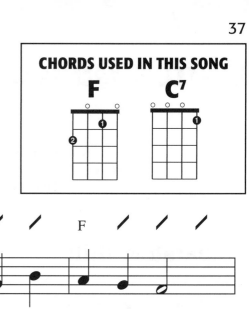

CHORDS USED IN THIS SONG
F    C⁷

Track 41 Melody & Chords    Track 42 Chords only

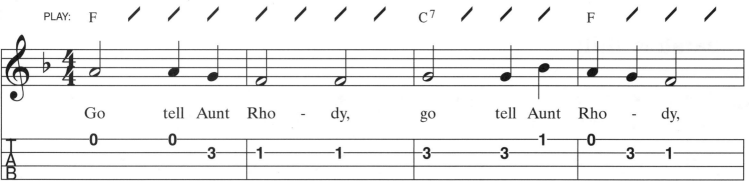

Moderato

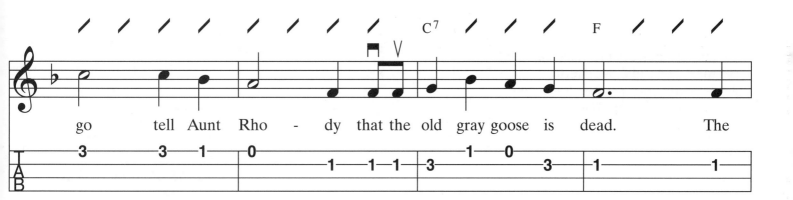

Go tell Aunt Rho - dy, go tell Aunt Rho - dy,

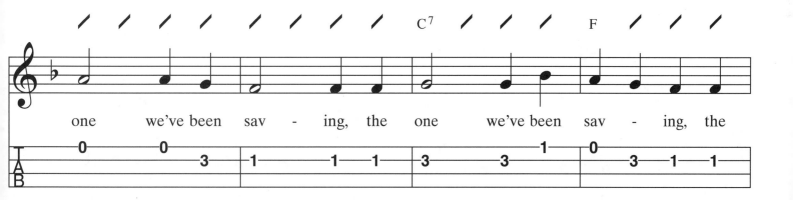

go tell Aunt Rho - dy that the old gray goose is dead. The

one we've been sav - ing, the one we've been sav - ing, the

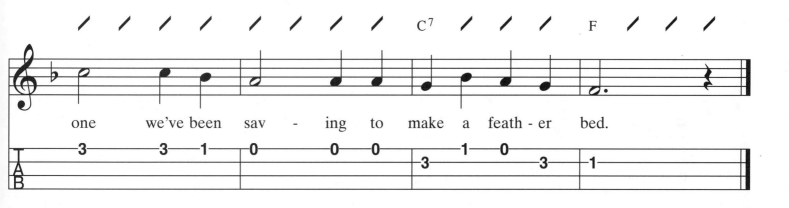

one we've been sav - ing to make a feath - er bed.

# Dotted Quarter Notes

A DOT INCREASES
THE LENGTH OF A NOTE
BY ONE HALF

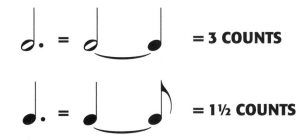

## Preparatory Drill

The only difference in the following two measures and those directly above them is the way they are written. They should sound the SAME.

## Cockles and Mussels

Track 43 Vocals & Chords
Track 44 Chords only

**CHORDS USED IN THIS SONG**
F    C⁷

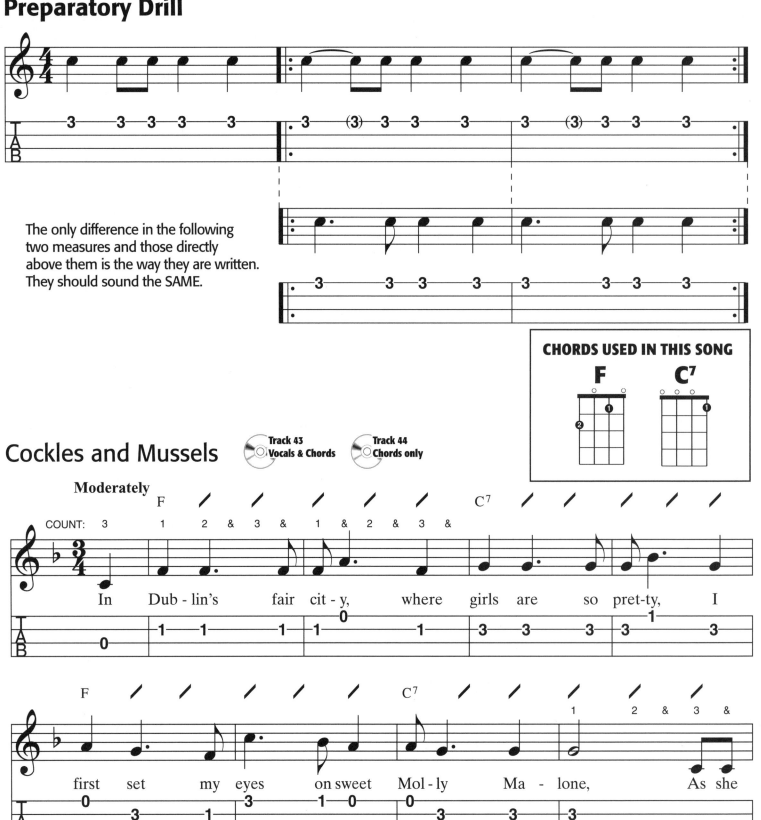

Moderately

COUNT: 3    1    2    &    3    &    1    &    2    &    3    &

In Dub-lin's fair cit-y, where girls are so pret-ty, I

first set my eyes on sweet Mol-ly Ma-lone, As she

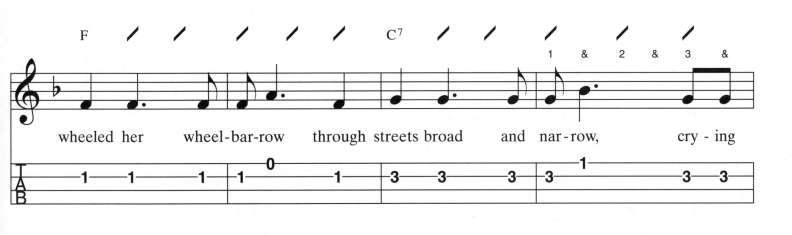

wheeled her    wheel-bar-row    through streets broad    and nar-row,    cry - ing

Cock - les    and    Mus-sels!    A - live,    a - live,    oh!

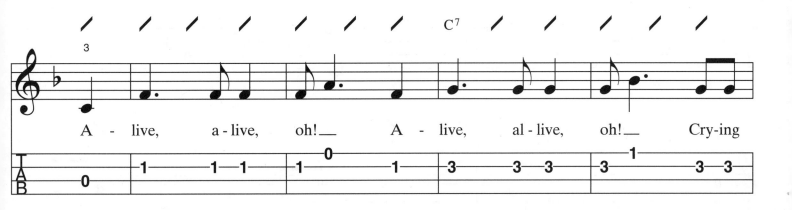

A - live,    a - live,    oh!__    A - live,    al - live,    oh!__    Cry-ing

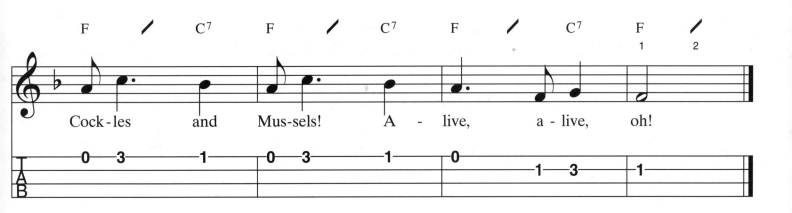

Cock - les    and    Mus-sels!    A - live,    a - live,    oh!

## Clementine

**Additional Verses**

*Verse 2:*

Light she was and like a fairy,

And her shoes were number nine,

Herring boxes, without topses,

Sandals were for Clementine.

*Chorus:*

Oh my darling, oh my darling,

Oh my darling Clementine!

Thou art lost and gone forever

Dreadful sorry, Clementine.

*Verse 3:*

Drove she ducklings to the water

Every morning just at nine,

Hit her foot against a splinter,

Fell into the foaming brine.

*Chorus:*

Oh my darling, oh my darling,

Oh my darling Clementine!

Thou art lost and gone forever

Dreadful sorry, Clementine.

*Verse 4:*

Ruby lips above the water,

Blowing bubbles soft and fine,

But, alas, I was no swimmer,

So I lost my Clementine.

*Chorus:*

Oh my darling, oh my darling,

Oh my darling Clementine!

Thou art lost and gone forever

Dreadful sorry, Clementine.

# The G7 Chord  Track 47

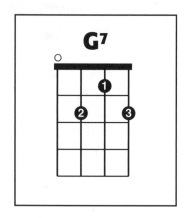

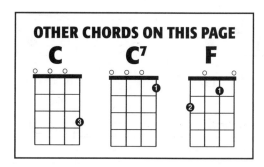

Place your 1st, 2nd, and 3rd fingers in position, then play one string at a time.

Play all four strings together:

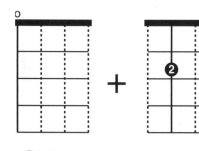 + 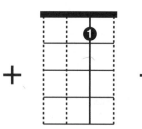 + 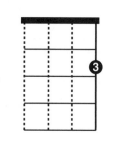 + 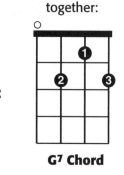 =

G7 Chord

Track 48

Play slowly and evenly.

1. 𝄞 4/4 G7 / / / | C / / / | G7 / / / | C / / / |

2. 𝄞 3/4 C / / | G7 / / | C / / | G7 / / | C / / | C 𝄼 𝄼 ‖

3. 𝄞 2/4 G7 / | C / | G7 / | C / | F / | C / | G7 / | C / ‖

4. 𝄞 4/4 C / / / | F / / / | C / / / | G7 / / / | C / / / | C / / 𝄽 ‖

5. 𝄞 3/4 C / / | C7 / / | F / / | C / / | F / / | F / / | C / / | C / / |

   G7 / / | G7 / / | C / / | F / / | C / / | C 𝄼 𝄼 ‖

**CHORDS USED IN THIS SONG**

F    C    C⁷    G⁷

# Aloha 'Oe  Track 49

(Farewell to Thee)

To get used to playing the G7 chord, play this version of "Aloha 'Oe" (pronounced "oy") with just chords.
Sing along with the melody.

This arrangement uses quarter note slashes ⌠ that indicate to play one strum on each quarter note.

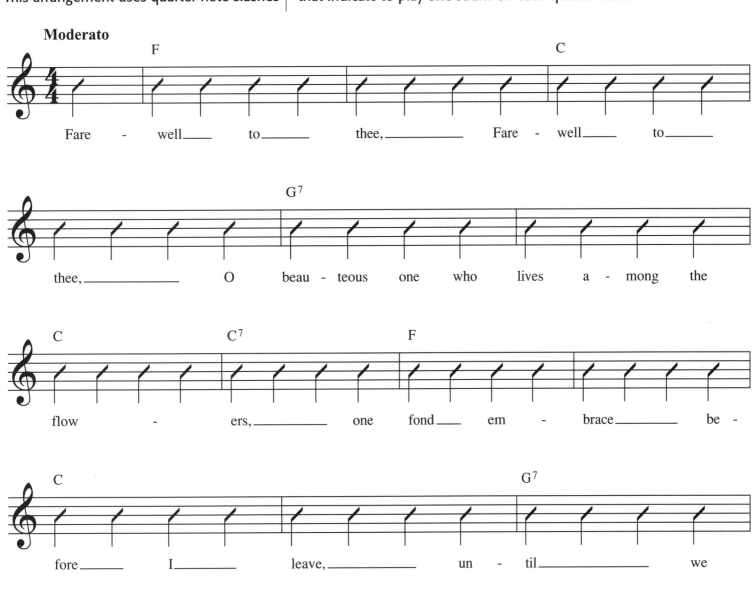

# When the Saints Go Marching In

# The Streets of Laredo

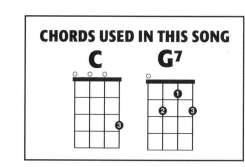

**CHORDS USED IN THIS SONG**

**Moderately**

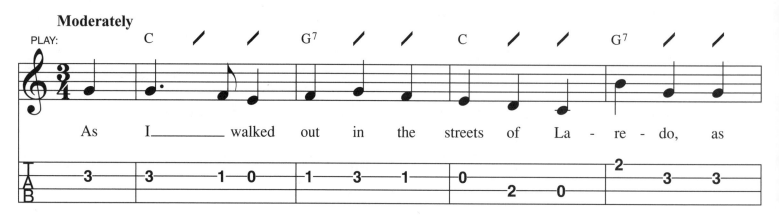

As I_____ walked out in the streets of La - re - do, as

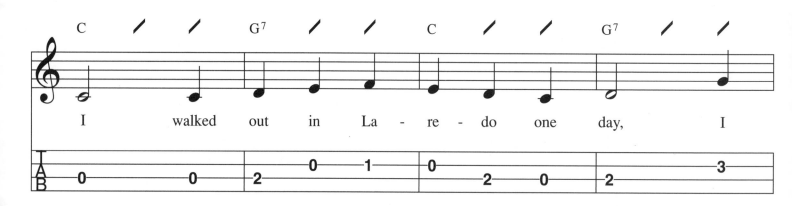

I walked out in Laredo one day, I

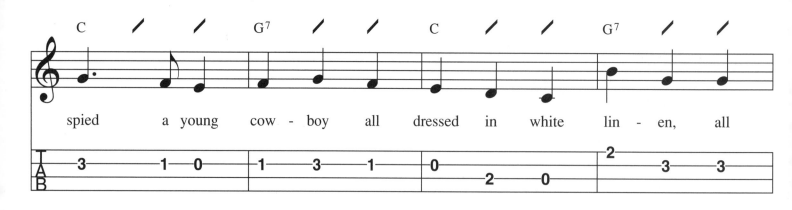

spied a young cow - boy all dressed in white lin - en, all

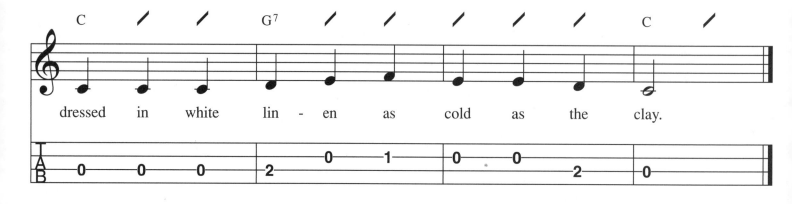

dressed in white lin - en as cold as the clay.

# The Down-and-Up Stroke  Track 56

You can make your accompaniment of waltz songs in $\frac{3}{4}$ like "The Streets of Laredo" more interesting by replacing the second beat of the measure with a down-stroke followed by an up-stroke. The symbol for down-stroke is ⊓; an up-stroke uses the symbol V. Together, the down-and-up strokes are played in the same time as a regular strum.

Try the following exercise to first just work on the new rhythm.

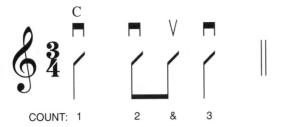

Now practice changing from C to G7.

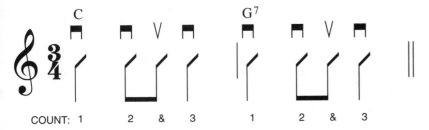

Now practice changing back and forth from C to G7 and back. When you can do it smoothly, go back to page 46 and use it to accompany "The Streets of Laredo."

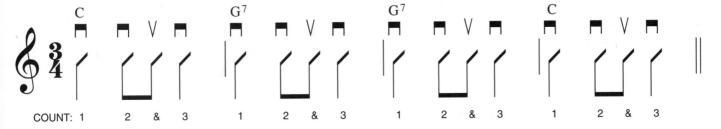

# The Fermata

This sign is called a *fermata*. It means to hold the note it is over a little longer.

**CHORDS USED IN THIS SONG**
C F G⁷

## Michael, Row the Boat Ashore

Track 57 Vocals & Chords

Track 58 Chords only

**Moderately slow and steady**

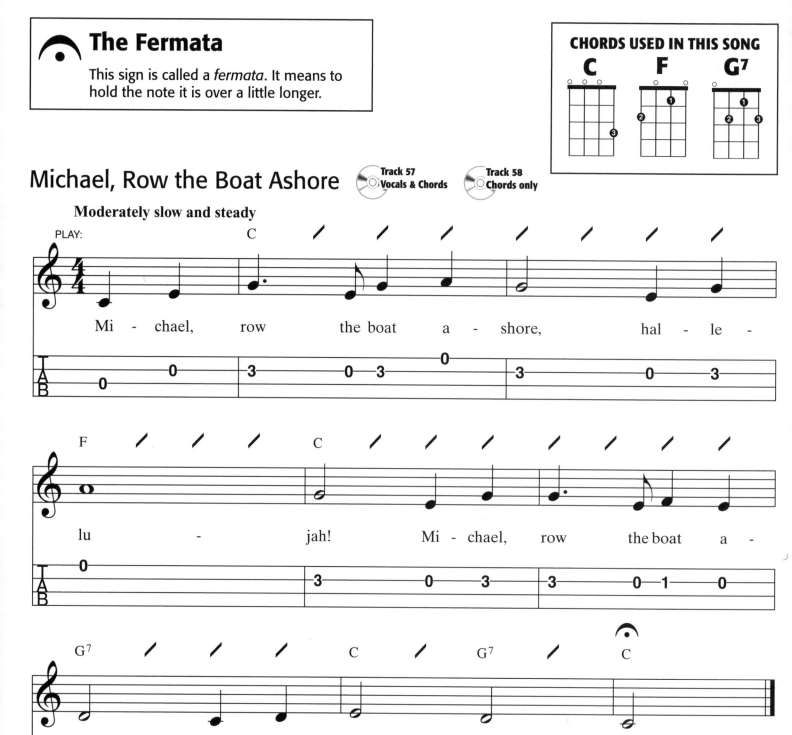

**Additional Lyrics**

*Verse 2*
Sister, help to trim the sail, hallelujah!
Sister, help to trim the sail, hallelujah!

*Chorus:*
Michael, row the boat ashore, hallelujah!
Michael, row the boat ashore, hallelujah!

*Verse 3:*
Jordan's river is chilly and cold, hallelujah!
Jordan's river is chilly and cold, hallelujah!

*Chorus:*
Michael, row the boat ashore, hallelujah!
Michael, row the boat ashore, hallelujah!

# The Dotted 8th and 16th Note Rhythm

Like 8th notes, dotted 8ths and 16ths are played two to each beat. But unlike 8th notes (which are played evenly) dotted 8ths and 16ths are played *unevenly*: long, short, long, short.

Compare the following:

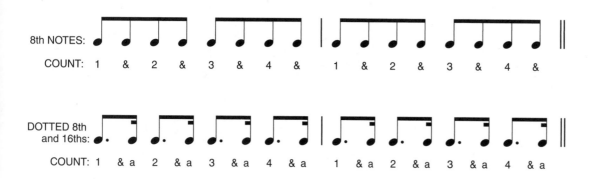

8th NOTES:
COUNT: 1 & 2 & 3 & 4 & 1 & 2 & 3 & 4 &

DOTTED 8th and 16ths:
COUNT: 1 & a 2 & a 3 & a 4 & a 1 & a 2 & a 3 & a 4 & a

An easy way to remember the sound of dotted 8ths and 16ths is to say the words:

"hump - ty dump - ty hump - ty dump - ty"

The dotted 8th and 16th note rhythm is very common in all kinds of music, but especially classical, folk, country, and blues. Here are examples of each to practice.

## Blues Strum  Track 61

You can make your accompaniment of songs like "Frankie and Johnny" more interesting by using a blues strum. Use the dotted 8th and 16th note rhythm. Each measure of $\frac{4}{4}$ time contains four down-strokes and four up-strokes.

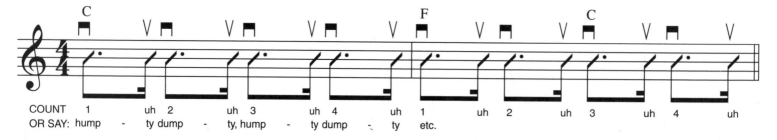

COUNT 1 uh 2 uh 3 uh 4 uh 1 uh 2 uh 3 uh 4 uh
OR SAY: hump - ty dump - ty, hump - ty dump - ty etc.

You can create a variation on the blues strum above by changing the notes on beats 1 and 3 to quarter notes so the rhythm is quarter followed by dotted 8th and 16th. Repeat this pattern twice in each measure.

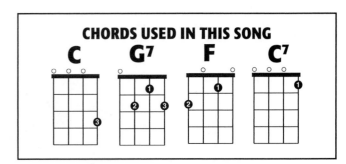

**CHORDS USED IN THIS SONG**
C    G⁷    F    C⁷

# Careless Love  Track 62

The blues strum will work nicely for this song. Notice the melody of "Careless Love" has notes you don't know. Many lead sheets you play from will contain notes that you can't play on the ukulele. If that is the case, just play the chords and sing along!

**Moderate blues tempo**

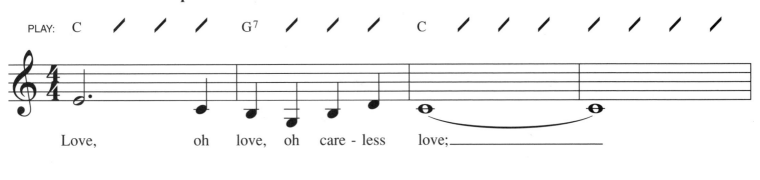

Love,           oh love, oh care - less    love;_____

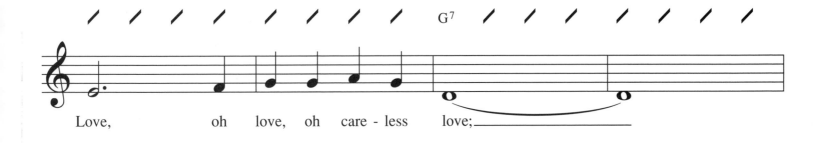

Love,           oh love, oh care - less    love;_____

Love,        oh love,        oh care - less        love;        just

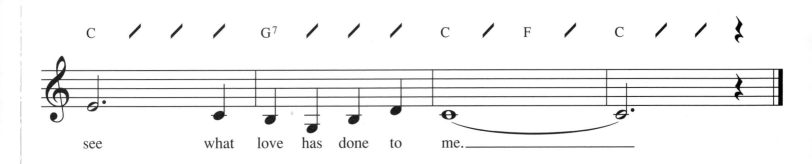

see        what  love  has  done  to    me._____

52

# The G Chord  Track 63

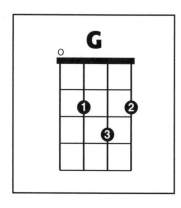 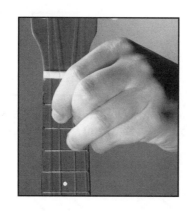

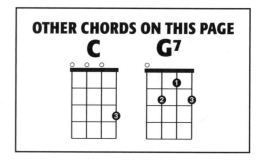

**OTHER CHORDS ON THIS PAGE**
C      G⁷

Place your 1st, 2nd, and 3rd fingers in position, then play one string at a time.

Play all four strings together:

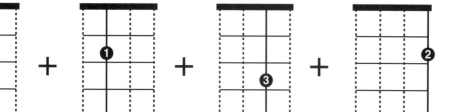

**G Chord**

 Track 64

Play slowly and evenly.

1. $\frac{2}{4}$ G  /  | G  /  | G  /  | G  /  | G  /  | G  /  ‖

2. $\frac{3}{4}$ G  /  /  | G  /  /  | G  /  /  | G  /  /  | G  /  /  ‖

 Track 65

Repeat each line several times.

1. $\frac{4}{4}$ G  /  /  / | G⁷  /  /  / | C  /  /  / | G  /  /  / ‖

2. $\frac{3}{4}$ G  /  / | G⁷  /  / | C  /  / | G⁷  /  / | C  /  / ‖

3. $\frac{2}{4}$ G  / | G⁷  / | C  / | G⁷  / | C  / | G  / | C  ⸴ ‖

# The D7 Chord

**Track 66**

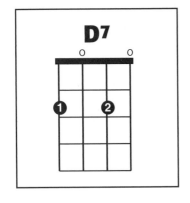

**OTHER CHORDS ON THIS PAGE**

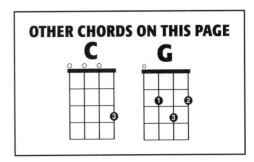

Place your 1st and 2nd fingers in position, then play one string at a time.

Play all four strings together:

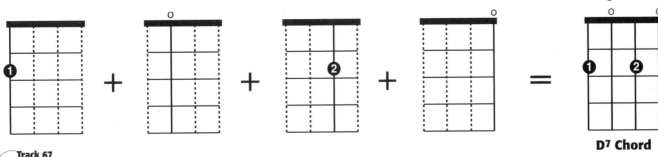

**D7 Chord**

**Track 67**

Play slowly and evenly.

1. $\frac{2}{4}$  D⁷ ╱ | D⁷ ╱ | D⁷ ╱ | D⁷ ╱ | D⁷ ╱ | D⁷ ╱ ‖

2. $\frac{3}{4}$  D⁷ ╱ ╱ | D⁷ ╱ ╱ | D⁷ ╱ ╱ | D⁷ ╱ ╱ | D⁷ ╱ ╱ ‖

**Track 68**

Repeat each line several times.

1. $\frac{4}{4}$  G ╱ ╱ ╱ | D⁷ ╱ ╱ ╱ | C ╱ ╱ ╱ | D⁷ ╱ ╱ | G ‖

2. $\frac{3}{4}$  G ╱ ╱ | C ╱ ╱ | D⁷ ╱ ╱ | C ╱ ╱ | G 𝄽 𝄽 ‖

3. $\frac{2}{4}$  G ╱ | G⁷ ╱ | C ╱ | D⁷ ╱ | G ╱ | C D⁷ | G ‖

# Introducing F-sharp

Track 69

A *sharp* ♯ raises a note a half step. F♯ is played one fret higher than the note F. When a sharp note appears in a measure, it is still sharp until the end of that measure.

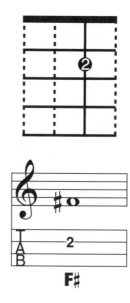

**F♯**

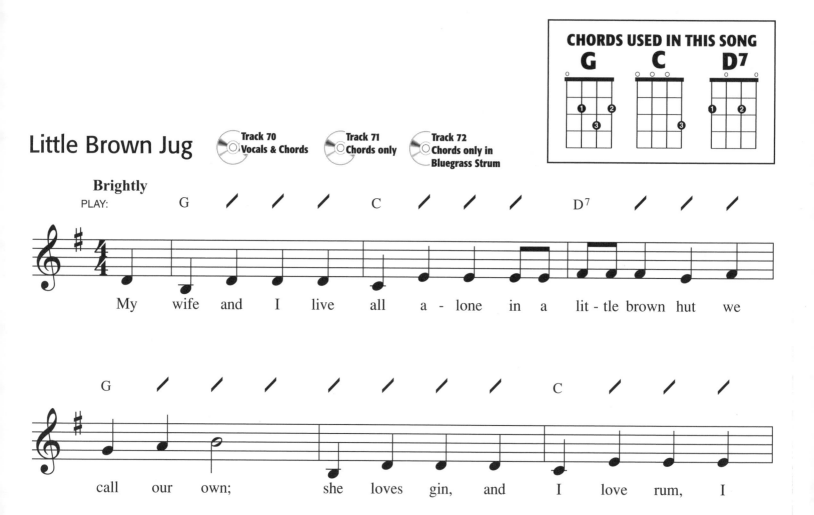

**CHORDS USED IN THIS SONG**

G    C    D⁷

## Little Brown Jug

Track 70 Vocals & Chords

Track 71 Chords only

Track 72 Chords only in Bluegrass Strum

**Brightly**

PLAY:  G  /  /  /  C  /  /  /  D⁷  /  /  /

My wife and I live all a - lone in a lit-tle brown hut we

G  /  /  /  /  /  /  /  C  /  /  /

call our own; she loves gin, and I love rum, I

tell you what, don't we have fun? Ha, ha, ha, you and me,

lit - tle brown jug, don't I love thee? Ha, ha, ha,

you and me, lit - tle brown jug, don't I love thee?

## Bluegrass Strum  Track 73

You can make your accompaniment to "Little Brown Jug" and other country favorites more interesting by using a bluegrass strum. This strum breaks up the steady four-beats-to-the-measure with up-strokes on the second and fourth beats. Try the exercise below, and when you can do it smoothly, apply it to "Little Brown Jug."

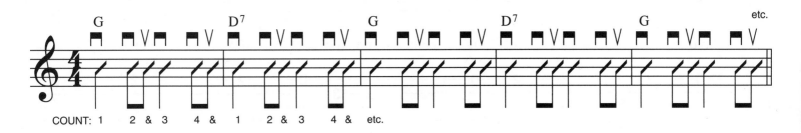

COUNT: 1 2 & 3 4 & 1 2 & 3 4 & etc.

# D.C. al Fine

*D.C. al Fine* stands for the Italian expression "Da Capo al Fine" (dah CAH-po al FEE-nay).
It means to go back to the beginning of the song and play as far as the word "Fine,"
which is the end of the song.

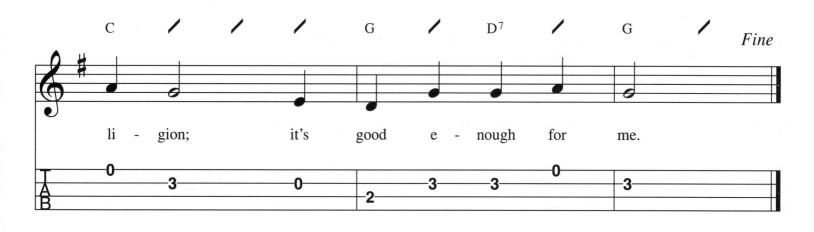

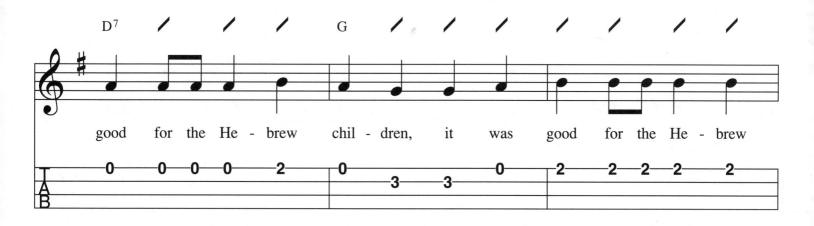

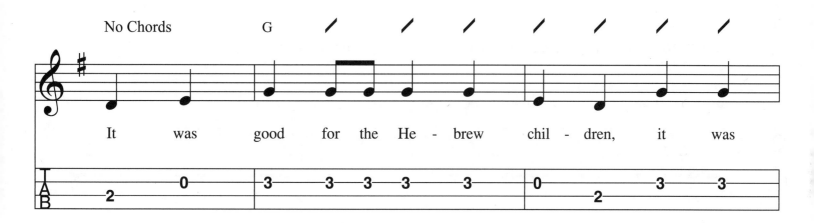

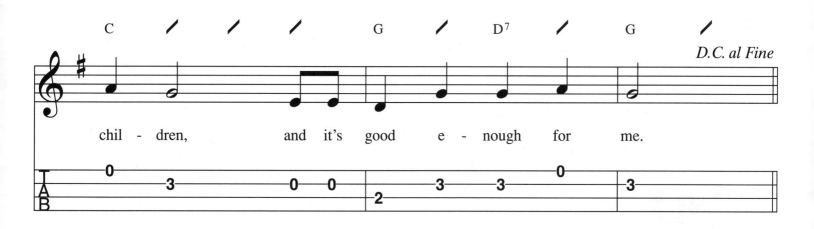

58

# Calypso Strum  Track 76

The calypso strum is used to accompany Caribbean songs like "Mary Ann," "Jamaica Farewell," and "The Sloop John B." The rhythm is a little tricky, so make sure you can play the exercises on this page before trying the songs.

Play a steady four-to-the-bar pattern on a C chord. Use only down-strokes.

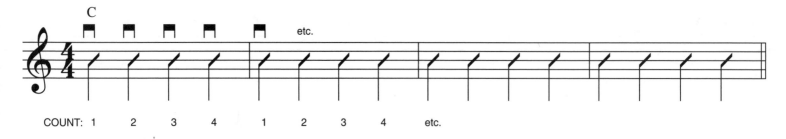

Now add an up-stroke after each down-stroke. Notice how the count has changed.

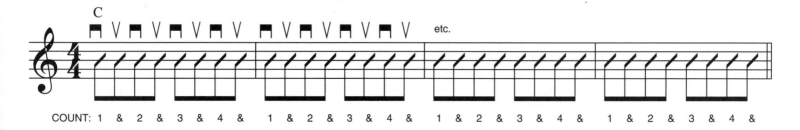

Now leave out the down-stroke on 3 and replace it with silence. Notice that you now have two up-strokes in a row on the "and" of 2 and the "and" of 3.

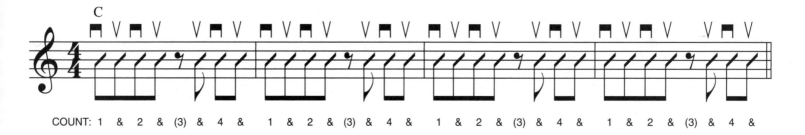

This whole pattern represents one measure of the calypso strum. As soon as you can do it without missing a beat, try "Mary Ann."

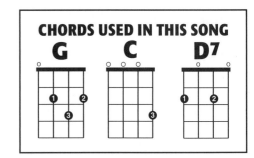

CHORDS USED IN THIS SONG
G    C    D7

## The Sloop John B.

Track 79
Vocals & Chords

Track 80
Chords only

Start this song with the calypso strum to get into the rhythm of it.
Then start singing.

**Moderately**

PLAY: G    C    D7    G

We

G

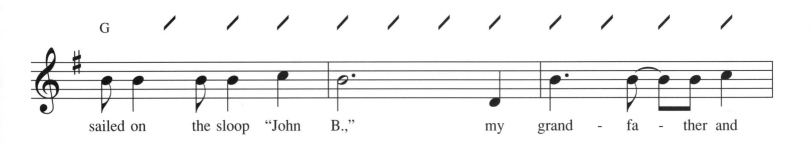

sailed on    the sloop "John    B.,"    my    grand - fa - ther and

me,    We    left    Nas - sau    Town    one    morn - ing    at

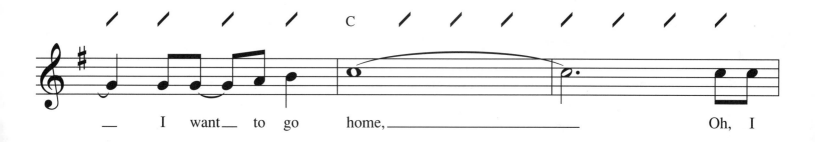

**Additional Verses**

*Verse 2:*
The first mate he got drunk, and broke the capn's trunk,
The constable had to come and take him away.
Sheriff John Stone, why don't you leave me alone?
Yeah, yeah. Well I feel so broke up, I wanna go home.

*Verse 3:*
The poor cook he caught the fits, and threw away all my grits
And then he took and he ate up all of my corn.
Let me go home, why don't they let me go home?
Yeah, yeah. This is the worst trip I've ever been on.

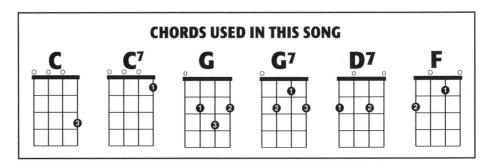

# Over the Rainbow

 Track 81

The greatest ukulele version of this song was recorded in 1993 by legendary Hawaiian uke player and singer Iz. This song will sound great with the calypso strum.

Words by E. Y. Harburg
Music by Harold Arlen

# CERTIFICATE OF PROMOTION

## ALFRED'S BASIC
## UKULELE METHOD 1

This certifies that

has mastered
Alfred's Basic Ukulele Method 1.

Teacher _____

Date _____